Forty-nine syllables on life

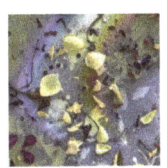

Other books

Photography: History, Art, Technique
Photography - the Definitive Visual History
Photo Judging
Picture Editing
Ang's World
Photo Field Guide
Creativity for Everyone
Digital Photography Step by Step
Digital Photography Essentials
Digital Photographer's Handbook
Complete Digital Photography
Questions & Angswers
Digital Photography: an Introduction
The Complete Photographer
Digital Photography Masterclass
Fundamentals of Photography
Digital Photography Through The Year
How To Photograph Absolutely Everything
Digital Photography
Tao of Photography
Eyewitness Companion: Photography
Picture Editing
Photoshop CS For Photography
Dictionary of Photography and Digital Imaging
Digital Photography
Silver Pixels
Kiss Digital Photography
Advanced Digital Photography
Complete Digital Photography
Private Album
Digital Video Handbook
Digital Video: An Introduction

As photographer
Marco Polo Expedition
Joy of Sex
General Wade's Roads
Dorset

Forty-
nine
syllables
on
life

**NUKU.
PRESS**

All text, images and book
2021 © Tom Ang

Images are from the
'Co-CREATION' series.

ISBN 978-0-473-55907-6

The author asserts his moral
rights over this work.

Published in New Zealand by
Nuku.Press an imprint of
AngBookCo Ltd.

Introduction

One day, I started writing poems. It was after my A-level exams, when the mind is stuffed full of school-book contents that suddenly have little utility and less meaning; when music all sound too slow; and hot, long days drain into a miasma of fear, confusion, frustration and troubled dreams.

But before long, I decided that free-form poems were too permissive, much too prone to encourage emotional drivel.

I tried haiku, but found the format too tight. After a year or so of experimentation - if you can call it that - more like self-indulgent rants and stutters, it came to me that a perfect square of syllables could work.

A count of twenty-five syllables made too tight a format as you had only five syllables per line to play with. And sixty-four was hard to sustain as well as being too prone to prattling in iambs. So I settled on forty-nine syllables: seven lines made up of seven syllables. Forty-niners.

It's of no great consequence that, as it happens, I write this some forty-nine years later. But neat is nice.

In that time, the forty-niners fell into two boxes. Loosely, and mostly for the sake of a label to put on them, those collected here are about life. The other collection is about love. The labels are about as illuminating as road names, so it's best not to put too much store by them.

At any rate, I dedicate both sets to Wendy, the glorious person who had the good sense to make me into what I am, the generosity to marry me, and has the patience to share life with me.

Tom Ang
Auckland
2021
www.tomang.com

1

What is the correct distance
to stand from life when with a
slip of focus our grasp of
reality sinks into
shadow leaving us to pluck
only ghosts of the day from
a future wholly unknown?

2

Indetermined arrivals
into life unannounced are
we early or always late
as significant as leaf's
irresolute lunge for earth
whose tremors sink into sand
awaiting evanescence.

3

Petty thoughts and the useless
fall out of minds as dust in
a slow sure rain of arid
mote on mote abrading each
other to the roundedness
of inconsequence drifting
to dead-ends but no settling.

4

Irreproducibles lie
in wait eager to harry
your search as your stumbling
on hopes in light-less corners
disturbs only just enough
to prove that sunny sides of
shadows are sham probably.

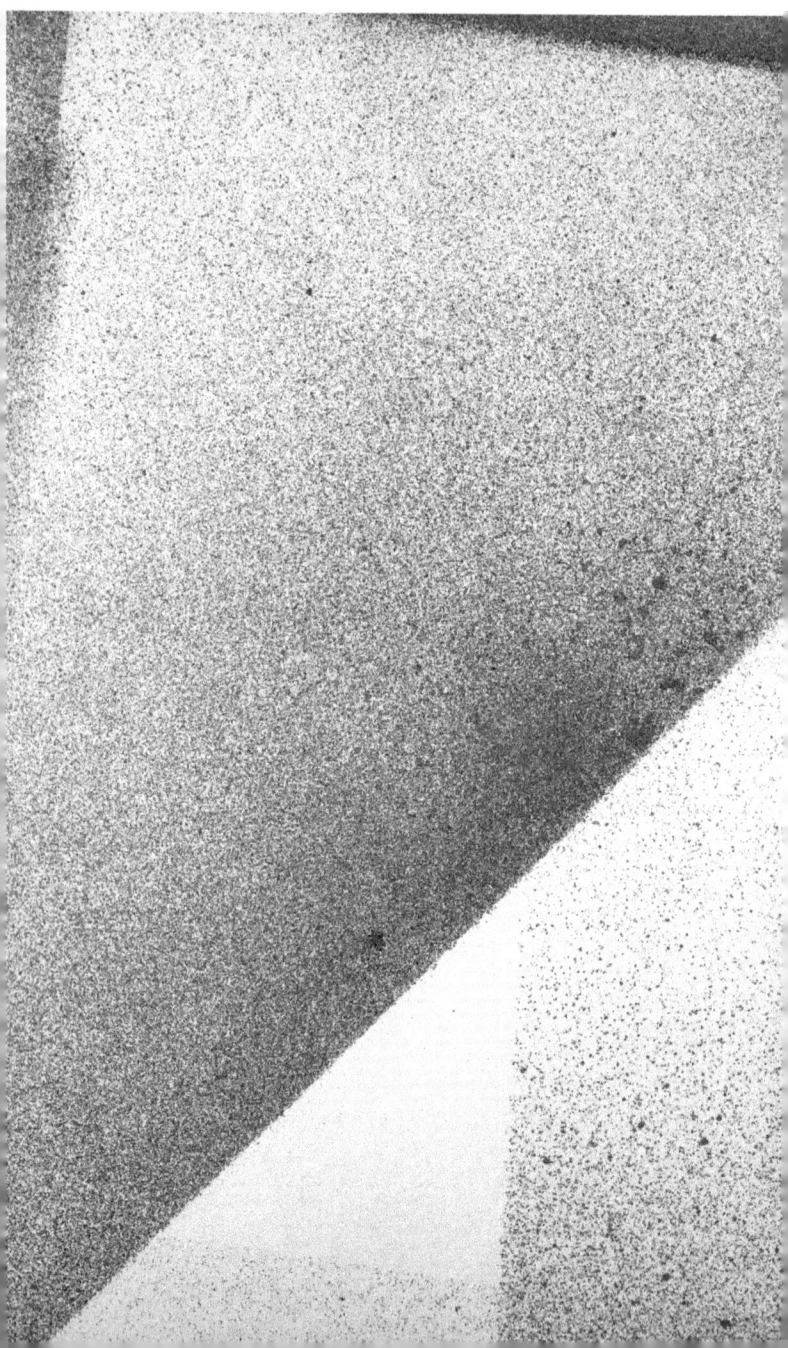

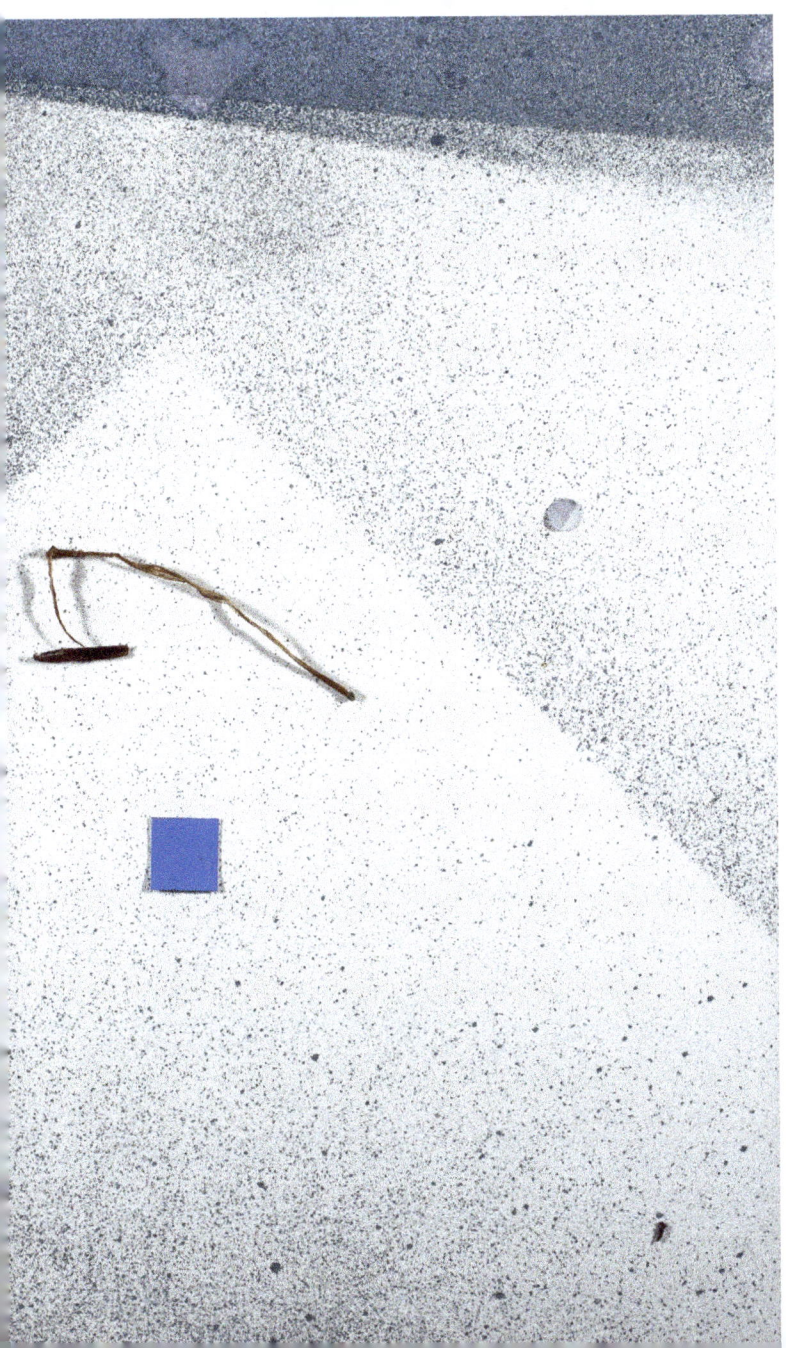

5

What search aims to find nothing
more present than the backward
calling for the never there
to counter the instant here
I shall look back with hot tears
to laugh at all the nows lost
to past dreams willed to return.

6

These arms cradle life's frail lines
but the anisotropy
of thought twists them mystified
by the simplicity of
truth's warmth it flails like grasses
wet with tears quaking in the
draught of future's arrival.

7

The songs of the desert groan
in sibilant keys as grain
grinds on grain like thoughts
lost in a billion-part fugue out
of step forever spinning
up the nose of the cosmos
to trigger celestial sneeze.

8

That the diaspora of
ideas are convolutions
of minds co-evolving to
union shows all are mingled
in the same Body so each
day's dawn must be a birthing
freshly renewing your breath.

9

When from the sweet business of
loving you I find leisure
as does bumble-bee submit
to ecstasies in pollen-
petalled profusion thus is
love-embedded repose such
an effortless state of grace.

10

Appogiatura of
crenate leaves trickles across
the outlines of our garden
in abundant verdance who
little-girl titter in the
slightest breeze strokes the fragrance
of peace that in-breath of life.

11

That light promises to point the
present yet persistently
lies in the past reshaping
clouds of hope to round off the
sharpest of resolutions
into grains rolling around
the desert's last syllables.

12

Soil dirt dust and the souls of
microbes convolve to blossoms
littering the sky while leaves
cover the grass-sute chest like
texts of love gravity-fed
into the myccorhizal
matrices one word a day.

13

Flecks of life these three could
dance on a point four at a
squeeze copulate in hairy
microscopy with pin-prick
accuracy finessed in
profligate detail tripping
over wind-swept molecules.

14

Obdurate tree roots ache their
way through rocks writing the first
staves of meaning well after
a century of sightless
longing in spaces between
thoughts whose depth of nothingness
measures wealth of potential.

15

In tumble-turning your mind
is a hawk's flick to dive slow
to a butterfly's life-path
a leaf in death flaps flakey
to the last it rests till a
thought stirs the past that flutters
back to its perch a flower.

16

This year may deafness decline
as shadows devolve from day's
ambiance by evaporating
to clouds of confusion to
such tension lighting must spark
ions to thunder brightly that
truth seen is spirit unbound.

17

You want to know you say but
are you ready to hear Truth's
white intensity that rounds
off all Existence to two
decimal places in the
process of proving that Time
is the Universe weeping?

18

Snake-smooth promises soil the
lease of truth to animate
trajectories of unease
like a trail of sodden steps
down the garden path to the
reveal and the loss that are
both sides of the sour sham.

19

This sonorous distraction
smelling of freshly warm bread
dawn-coloured distrubs the neat
scripts needed by truth's attempt
to ring like the sun's bell but
there's less life in certainty
than swift sea-breeze embraces.

20

Whispers slick across moon beams
uneasy on seas rich in
ancient groans and sleeplessness
then limp in doleful search for
frothy signs in the waves should
sibilant splashes map the
desolation helpfully.

21

To slip from paradise berth
your arms in whose safety is
final danger for some source
shimmering with the promise
of a sunbeam partying
over a threshold washed smooth
by tears will take some doing.

22

Nowness is a song fading
even as it sways through the
right ventricle en route to
its rummage of wisdom's bin
storing all the travails from
a long-gone locus back to
the start whence once becomes now.

23

An ebullience of rotund
rocks flings light about in jigs
free-tumbling around the all-
sparkling baubles carelessly
ceaseless the streams' babbling
is purest music having no
not meaning yet all beauty.

24

Tone-deaf to the inflections
of beach-fondling foam-flaked waves
does canned music stomp a path
to a raucous wind-dried to
vacuous as consonant with
tide rise of moon-falls as baby
wipes are beach-comber trophies.

25

Scalding even the sun your
smile doubles the day's beauty
making sky-beams frizzle in
watery murmuration
whose threats to wind-puff to naught
is delight's intransigence
a cheerful oxymoron.

26

Your majestic ease must
drip by rain-drop be bought with each
storm-proven root's attrition
of space grain by grain gained to
bind free energy into
sculptures whose effortless stance
rises from ceaseless effort.

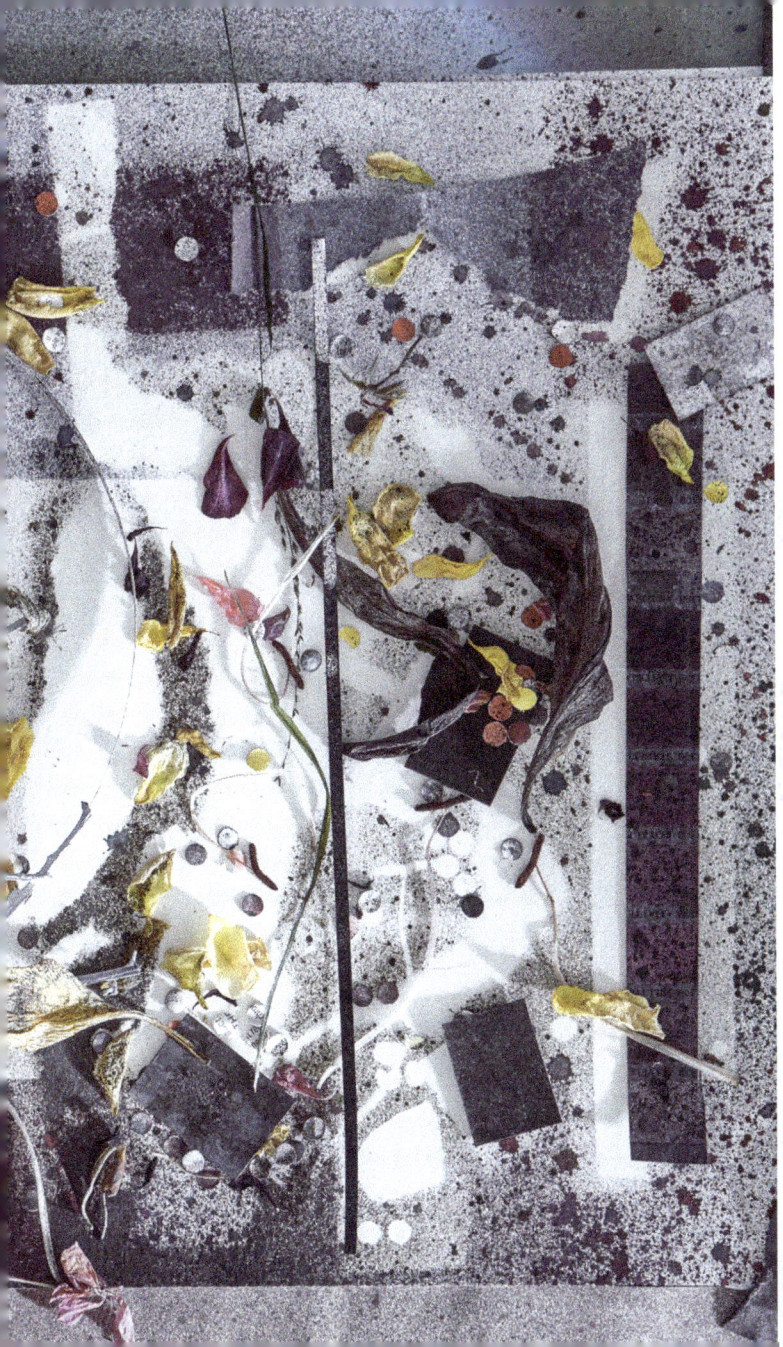

27

Mundanities will make dull
much light whose gyrations bore
until a beam by random
flight alighting flames dust to
cynosure showing us that
beauty is a sonorous
distraction from drab heart-beat.

28

Immersion in chatter seeks
solace from baleful silence
as the vacuous will reveal
less of self than leaves flicking
shadows on and off for a
dozing tree's dream is woven
from strands of wind one year long.

29

The comfort of certitude
makes words play shadow tag on
damp-streaked walls enclosing a
church of chimaeras that are
projections from torch-bearers
unaware they've been blinded
by the light of their own truths.

30

Silken songs of stream revel
in heat-spun laceries lights
staccato-tongue the ripples
aiming for the blue depths skies
dive in grateful for cool peace
where leaves waltz silently in
gyratory harmonies.

31

Light makes airy promises
with hints of glamour that the
italic version in your
eyes is starlight rendered gives
us little-needed proof that
beauty lies in catching the
ordinary by surprise.

32

Melodious thoughts are the gifts
of the god of grass blades though
closed to skimming sight they are
soul-filling should pride's power
be shed in fugacious leaf-
fall to ensure that hubris
strikes only the most worthy.

33

That cold yet fingers distant
years through desert heat and chill
even jungle sweat means it
lies in wait beneath layers
of thought-fallen debris that
ring-bark healing for journeys
are long when warmth is denied.

34

Driven by the desire
for order that is relief
from change if only briefly
suspended life weaves space with
light in the betweenness whence
all things emerge limp and damp
into the sunlight blinking.

35

Let's now unpetal these lies
since brights and shadows devolve
life's dwindling secrets you can
scale chromatic harmonies
to unzip blue skies from clouds
then may you sun yourself in
music of truth-telling light.

36

When new thinking cringes to
curl circinnate the throb of
day's pulses are unfolding
of fronds paused only for dusk's
disrobing in ritual start
to dreams soon to be more real
than the life they comment on.

37

Life's escapement is driven
by the concuspicence of
every moment's failing breath
leaving the past to claw for
the present without which we'd
all be dust by now which is
why we're here to be grateful.

38

In the space that lies between
empty and nothing the pain
of disunion leads to life's
first intake of breath that will
rouse the stars to crochet with
the strands of time but leave holes
for light to return safe home.

39

Passing over the before
with an unhelpful glare and
dismissing the after with
an abrogative stare all
memories are but death masks
of their moments that set to
conceal more than they reveal.

40

Day-long do years undulate
not as arrows but wisps of
time ignored in the main they
elide space and thought as they
wait for the big cadence to
resolve but for change there is
always living to be done.

41

Mis-wafted midge-clouds of thoughts
are drift-in-wind desires
in futile dance to lift up
the setting sun believing
yet in the impossible
without which there can be no
faith in anything at all.

42

Querulous through dew-thick air
flick the crystal-flakes of song
scratching paths through the silence
in mists with dank to unload
a bird shivers then trills now
emphatic but falters soon
fading fast to insouciance.

43

As silence of the standing
people measures our deafness
to heart-beats slower than a
tuatara's breathing so do
leaves that flick to every jog
and Brownian jig on branching
articulations of sky.

44

When windless waves lean limp to
shore swimming on the surface
of silence it is time to
listen for the voice will grow
softer as her power gains
thus we must learn nature's love
is loudest when she whispers.

45

The granulairty of
life resists the elisions
of poetry whose sloppy
semantic habits are apt
to disarm differences well
isn't that such a relief
from stadial patriarchy.

46

Memory valley-folds time
facing in-take to out-breath
and obversely floats blue sky
hope turned away from roots worked
in darkness for the now stays
poor till sorrows from the past
become steps to the future.

47

Gorgeousness glows no less if
it is never gazed on but
a melody unheard makes
a rustling in life's casual
locus whose meanders are
subsumed by the headlong thrust
of time's rush for its own end.

48

A flux of sun lances through
voids too barren to be seen
until negotiating a
shoal of gaps it colours that
blossoming of sexual flaunt
it has flown a hundred and
fifty million clicks for.

49

Come sit lightly with me so
we may observe clouds transcribe
time's monologue as she combs
her rounds like a leaf breeze-tipped
will drip into polished pool
to radar out ripples in
search for echoes from afar.

www.ingramcontent.com/pod-product-compliance
Lightning Source LLC
Chambersburg PA
CBHW062028290426
44108CB00025B/2828